CHILDREN'S BOOK COUNCIL EXHIBIT
MISSOURI STATE LIBRARY

A Friend Can Be

written and illustrated by **CAL ROY**

AN ASTOR BOOK / Astor-Honor, Inc., New York

© Copyright 1969 by Astor-Honor, Inc.

Printed in the United States of America. All rights reserved. No part of this book may be used or reproduced in any manner whatsoever without written permission except in the case of brief quotations embodied in critical articles and reviews. For information address Astor-Honor, Inc., 26 E. 42nd Street, New York, N.Y. 10017.

LIBRARY OF CONGRESS CARD NO. 69-19191

FIRST PRINTING

A
Friend
Can Be

What is a friend?
Someone I know,
a voice to whom I say hello,
a face
and eyes I'm glad to see,
hands that
happily
like me.
Although
a friend can also be . . .

. . . a Lion

He walks like wildfire,
sits like the sun—
kitten and king and sphynx
in one.

. . . a Fish

Fleck of topaz,
flame of fin,
out the shy fish flashes.
In.

. . . a Mouse

The mouse is king
below the stairs,
lord of cellar smells
and pears half rotten,
nibbled strings
on things forgotten,
things for which
nobody cares.

But do mice ever laugh
below the stairs?

. . . a Fly

A spider spins a silken eye
that envies the Tiffany wings
of a fly.

A spider spins a silken ear
that envies the lighthearted songs
it hears.

A spider spins a silken mouth.
But I've warned the fly,
and that's enough.

. . . a Bee

Sunflower slurring,
whirring bee,
puffy,
purring
peony.

... a Tree

The tree has magic hands
that entertain the year—
turn green to red,
cause leaves and birds to disappear,
and beckon
on those birdless nights
the milk-cheeked moon,
to hold her near.

. . . a Mountain

In a room
I feel the walls'
embrace.
On a mountaintop
I'm hugged by
space.

...a Songbird

A robin hidden
in the green
bursts into song,
and I have seen
a summer palace built between
the first note's sparkle
and the last note's sheen.

. . . a Snowbird

A ghost of song,
an autumn puff of feathers
in a wintry show,
my silent sparrow weathers
long nights, rough storms,
to eat his breakfast
from a tablecloth of snow.

. . . a Seabird

In creaks
he speaks
to whales
and sails.
He skims
the shark-finned
wind of gales
that shaves
the waves
and drifts
the mist before.
He wishes
fishes
into food.
He mews
the news
in billowy mood.
His feet
leave neat
impressions
on the shore.
The weathered
feathered
peaceful
man o' war.

... a Frog

> Remember the frog
> with eyes like blintzes
> who lived in a well
> and married a princess?

Who taught me to dive?
Who taught me to swim?
Who taught me that nothing's impossible?
Him.

. . . a Fantasy

Wings of jade
flash my window shade.
"Dream safe," they said.

Or was it the flight
of a falling star?
The sudden lights
of a passing car?
Who knows
what firebirds
really are?

. . . the Sun

The sun on my back
is a snake that bites.
The sun in my eyes
is a tree of lights.

. . . the Wind

The wind is a secret.
But try to keep it!

The wind is disaster. . .
and a dancing master.

. . . a Shower

In summer it's fun
to lash down lanes
and run into pools
with your hand
in the rain's.

... the Fog

Silent on fog-feet,
muffled in capes,
followed by foghorns,
shadowing shapes,
the fog and I float...
what exciting time spent,
misting through cities
on secret assignment!

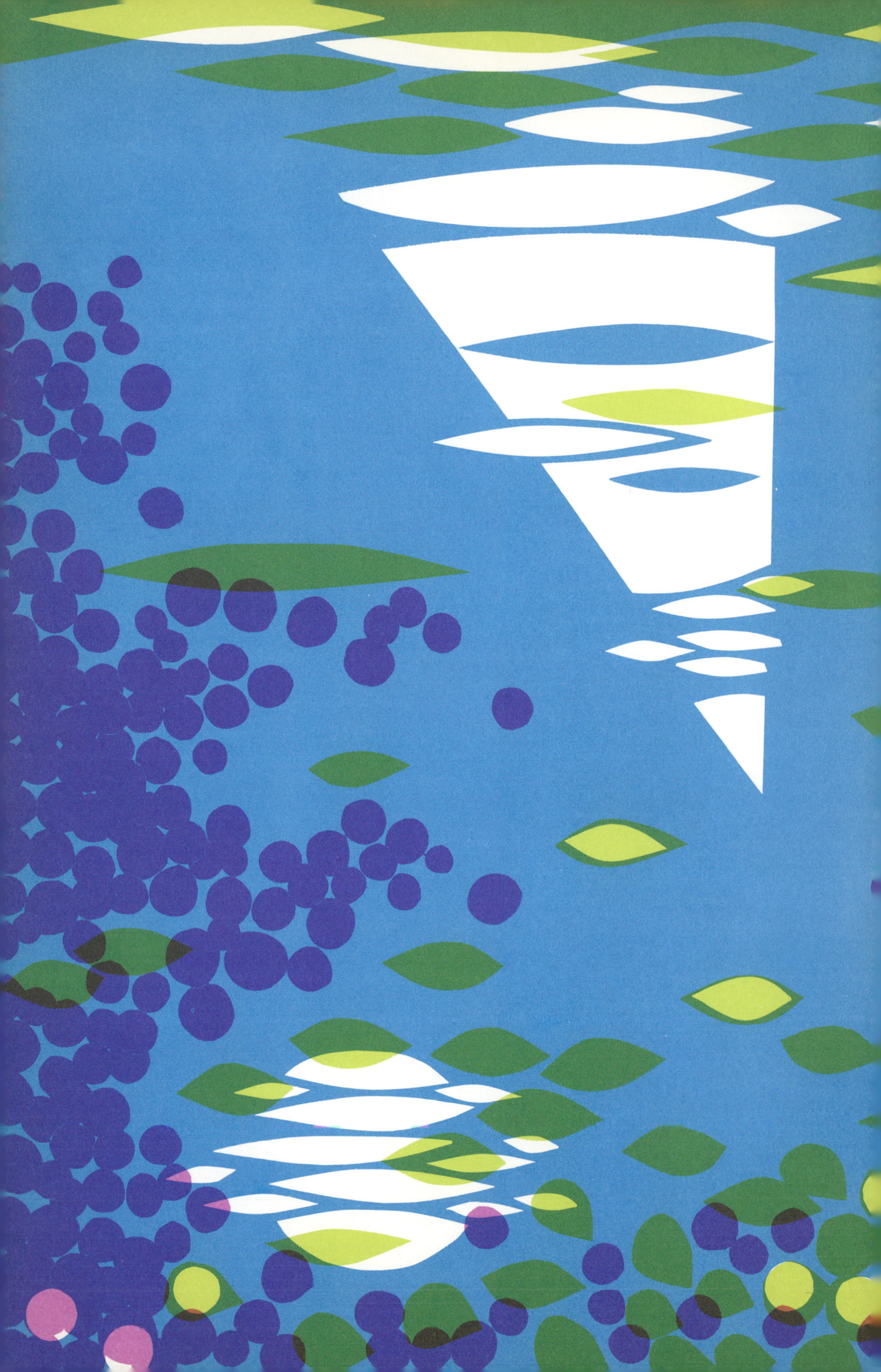

... a Boat

A boat
is to float
on pictures of sails,
on shadows,
on sun-gold,
on waterbug trails,
on minnows,
on trees growing
upside down.

A boat
is to float
up the summer
and down.

. . . a Kite

It clings to the wings
of the wildest wind.
Its strength flows the length
of the string in my hand.

Small as a leaf,
a thousand feet high,
my kite *is* my hand
on the heart of the sky.

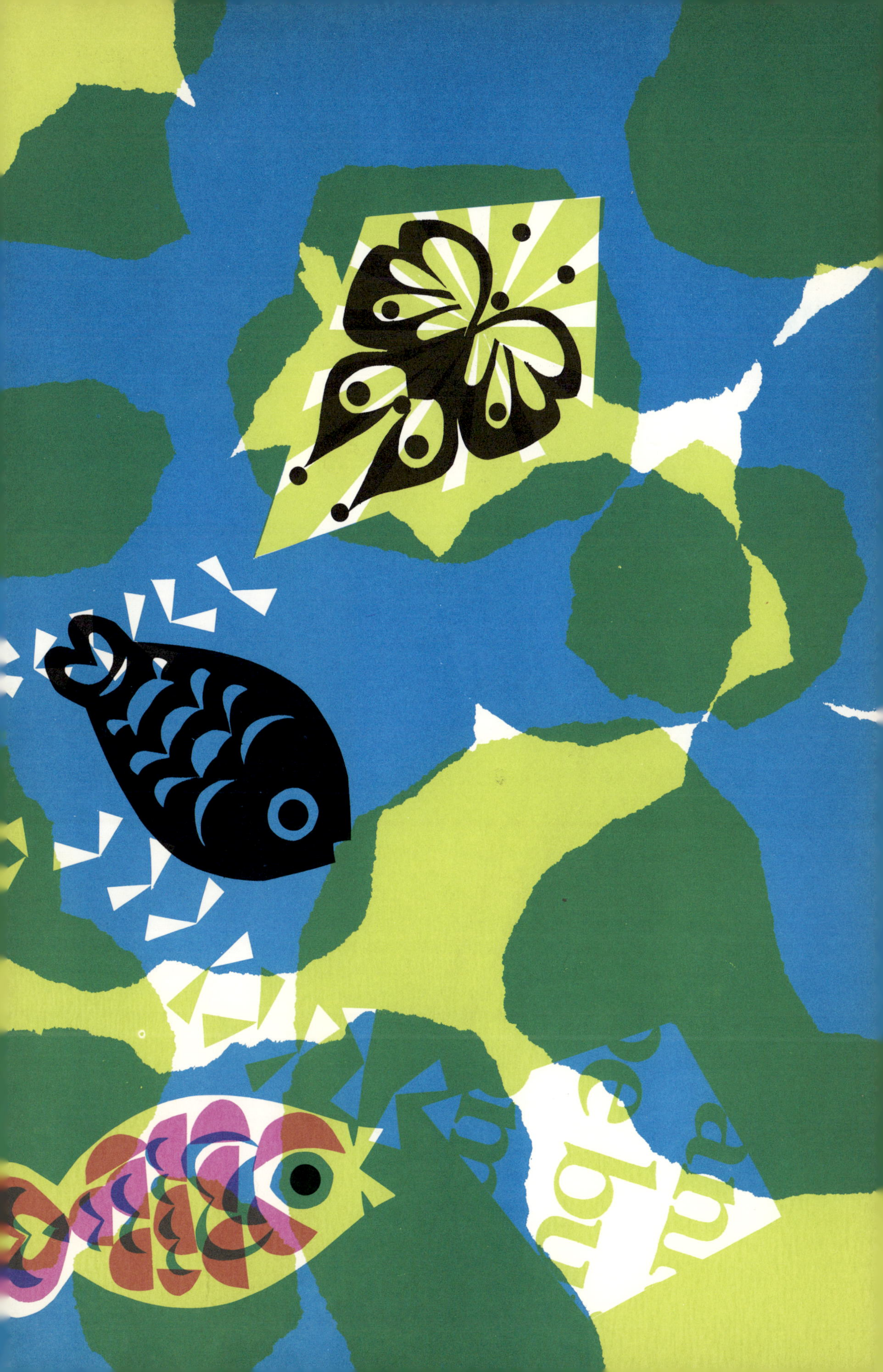

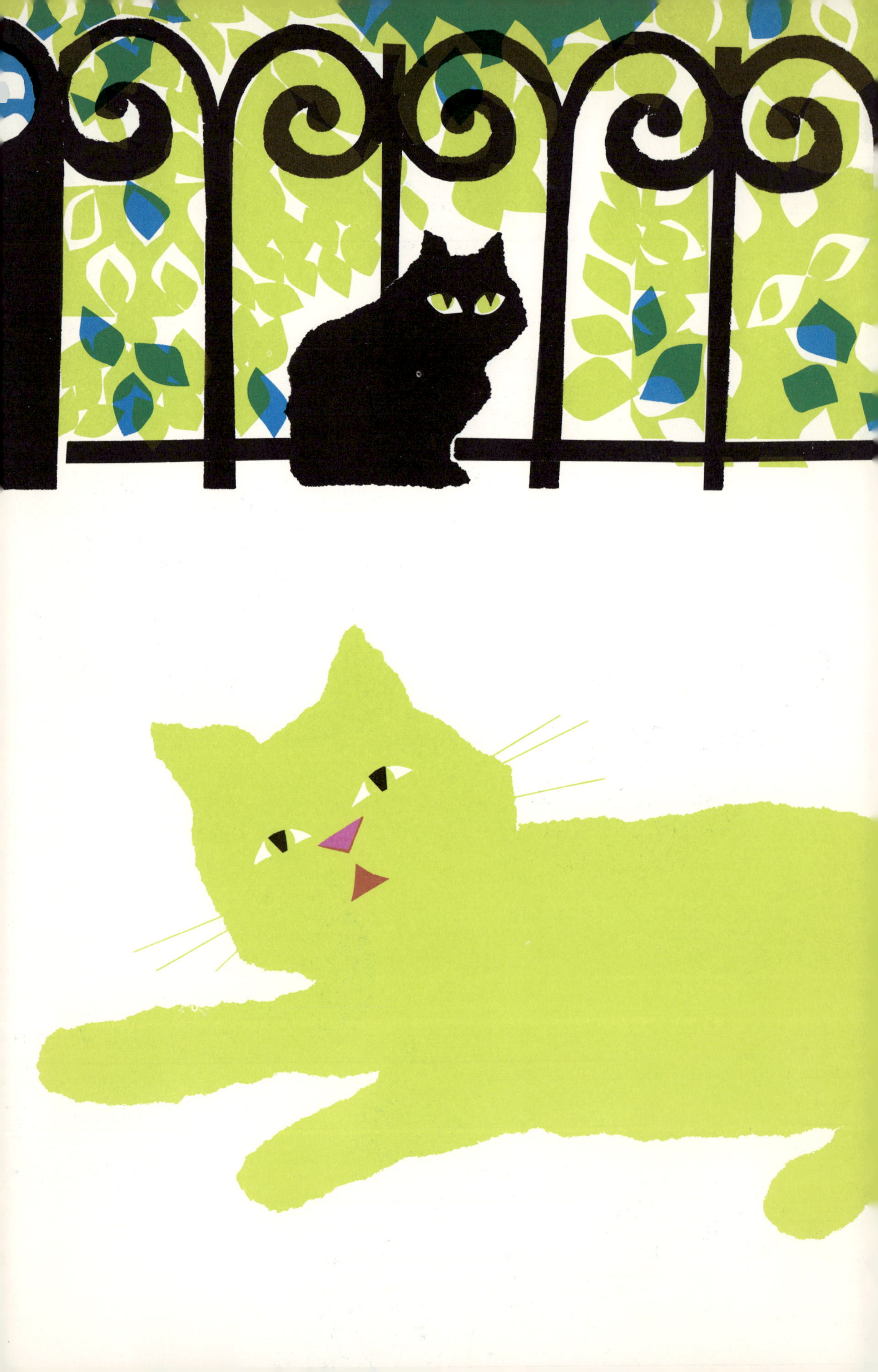

... a Cat

I forget,
have you met
my neighbor Othello?
He's pepper black,
Desdemona's yellow.
We're quite good friends.
They're nice.
But twice
I caught them kidnapping
the king of the mice.
One must expect that.
A cat's a cat.

. . . Night

It's dark now,
soft and still
and deep as earth.
The dark's a hill
to cross to sleep.
I roll down gentle slopes,
then steep,
and somersaulting,
sink to rest
on night,
on dream,
on hill,
on breast.

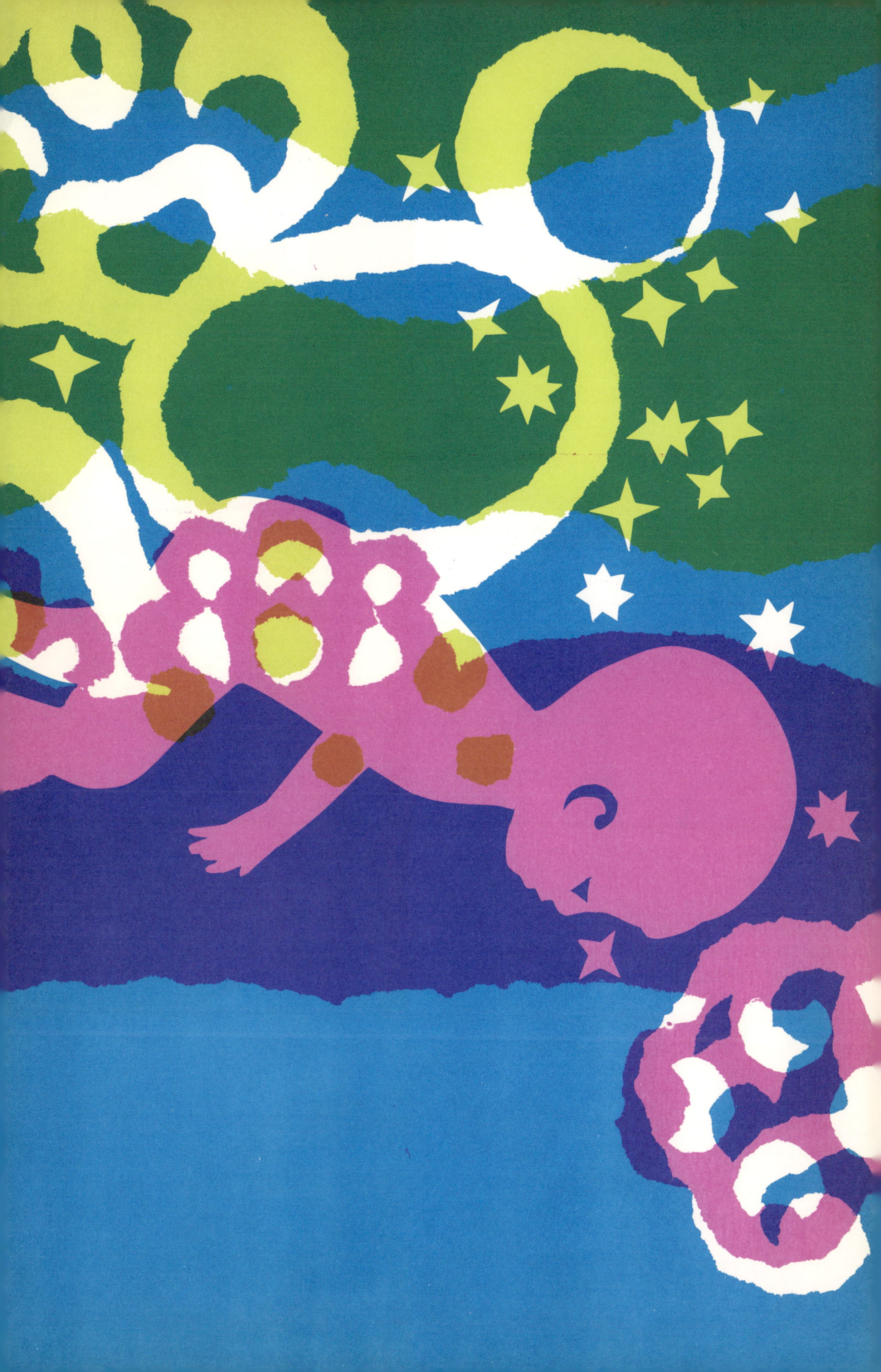

And so
a friend can be a bee,
a frog,
the fog,
a fantasy,
a fish,
a fly,
a shower,
a tree,
a kite,
a cat,
the night,
the sun
and anyone
or anything
whose being
is a happening.

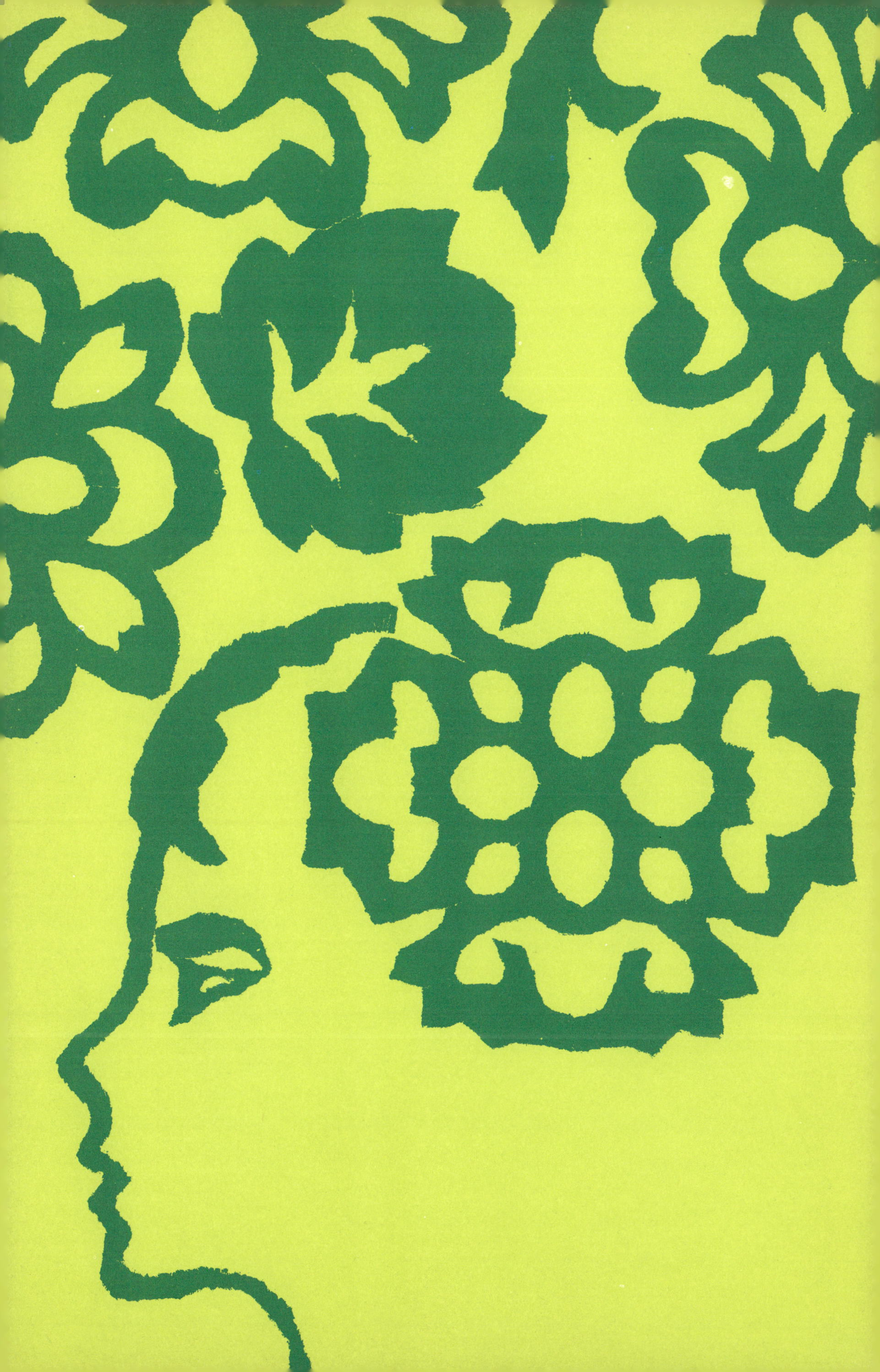

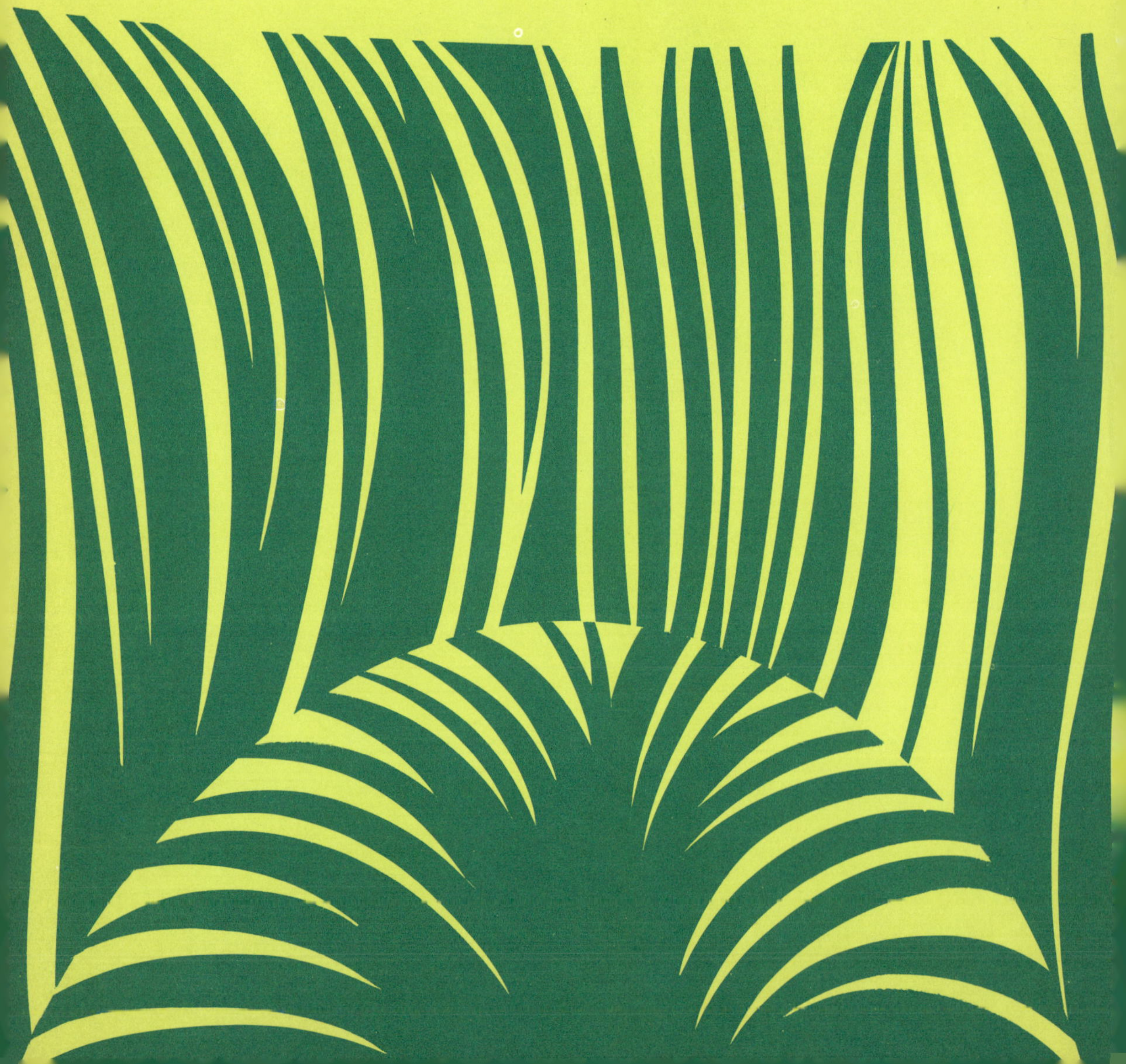

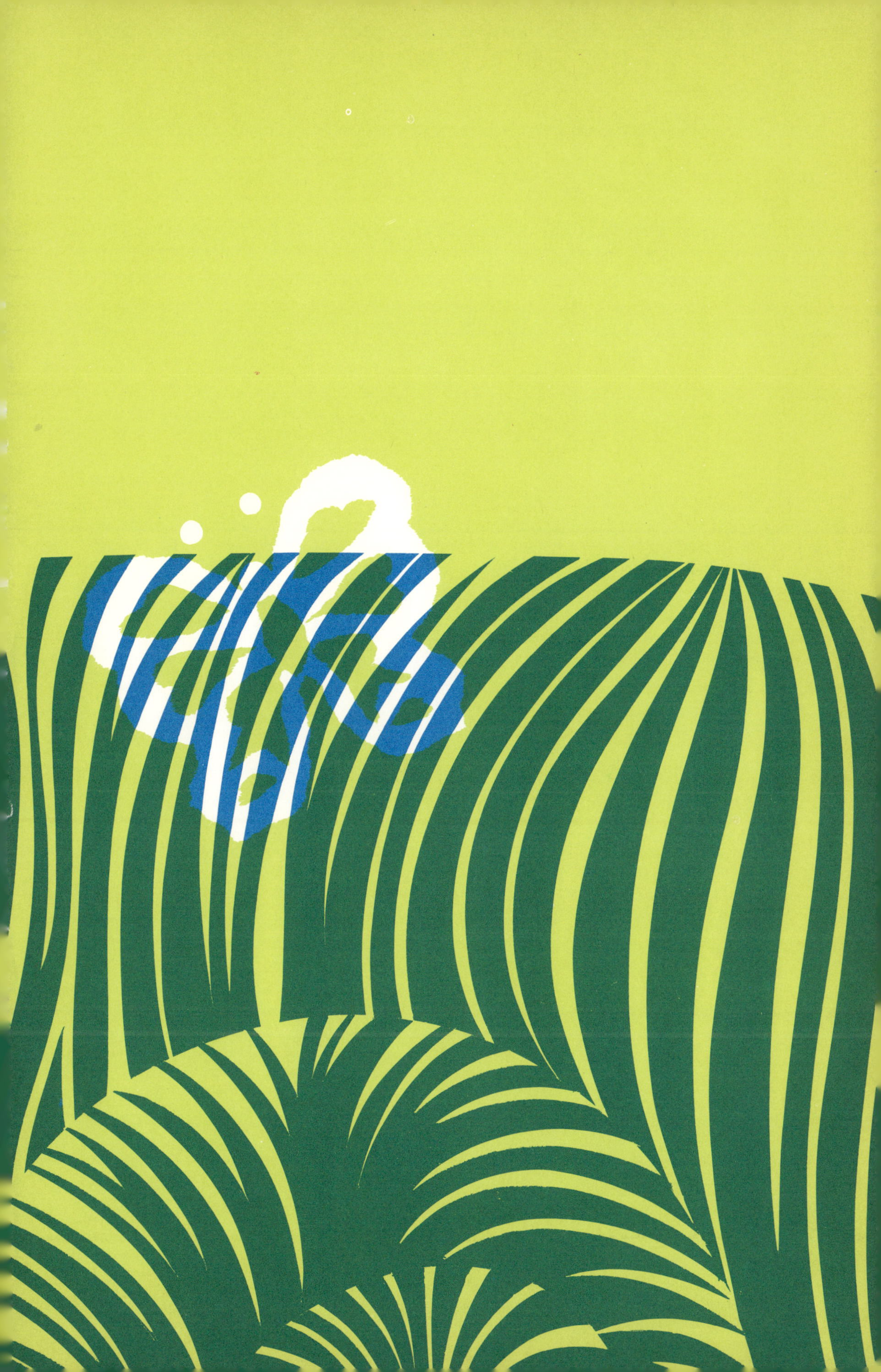